Blissful

✤ Bites

Turning full-size recipes into bite-size portions

Praise for Blissful Bites

Ashley may not be singing to my kiddos on our doorstep every Sunday, but they are singing her praises from our kitchen. Actually, I'm the one singing her praises. Even as a food blogger, I have a houseful of picky eaters, but I've got two secrets that slowly change those picky eaters into foodies, even if it takes years. Those secrets are to get them cooking and to make their food bite-sized. Ashley has a way of sweeping into the hearts of people with her happy personality and recipes. Sitting at the counter with my littles and picking from an array of tantalizing recipes is turning our weeknights into sweet, happy moments instead of whining chaos. The stories and recipes are simply perfect, whether you're a momma just trying to get your toddler to try one bite, or a seasoned cook waiting for the grandkids to show up for a holiday meal.

—Carrian, author of *Oh, Sweet Basil*

I am a professional pastry chef and have worked in the wedding industry for over ten years. When I was told about this new cookbook, I knew I was going to love it just by seeing the cover. *Blissful Bites* is the perfect roadmap to making the perfect, small-sized foods and desserts to serve at any occasion. If you are in need of some fresh food inspiration or just want to collect a new cookbook, *Blissful Bites* is the way to go. I love this book and the author herself! I most definitely recommend it for anyone in the market for a new cookbook.

—Whitney Berge, the Blonde Who Bakes

I am totally in love with this cookbook! It's all about the way we eat today. Gone are the days when we sat down to a regular meal of meat, potatoes, and vegetables. Today we like to eat smaller portions with lots of different tastes, and this book hits the mark with sweet, savory, and everything in between! Ashley has always been one of the best cooks I know, but her skill at stylish presentations of small bites will be appreciated by everyone, especially the home cook who likes to entertain with ease. Three cheers for Ashley's first Cookbook, which will be treasured by both home and professional cooks, and thank you, Ashley, for making the fine art of hors d'oeuvres so comfortable!

—Mary Crafts, founder Culinary Crafts

Blissful Bites is full of delicious, made-from-scratch recipes for any level baker. I love how Ashley makes the process of cooking and baking so approachable. Her passion and love of food exude from every page of this book.

—Courtney Rich, Cake by Courtney

Blissful Bites has completely changed the way I entertain. Guests simply enjoy "bites." Not only are they entertaining and fun for the adults, but the children and young people also adore them. "Bites" inherently bring a foodie atmosphere to the table. True to form, Ashley's food once again carries the party on its back and takes the pressure off the event. I'm so happy to have this book in my kitchen! It didn't take long before I inducted it into my cooking Hall of Fame!

—Hannah Neeleman, Ballerina Farm

ISBN 13: 978-1-4621-3770-1

Published by Front Table Books, an imprint of Cedar Fort, Inc.
2373 W. 700 S., Springville, UT 84663
Distributed by Cedar Fort, Inc., www.cedarfort.com

Library of Congress Control Number: 2020940413

Cover design by Shawnda T. Craig
Page design by Shawnda T. Craig
Cover design © 2020 Cedar Fort, Inc.

Printed in the United States of America
10 9 8 7 6 5 4 3 2 1

Printed on acid-free paper

Blissful ⊹ Bites

Turning full-size recipes into *bite-size portions*

Front Table Books
An imprint of Cedar Fort, Inc. • Springville, Utah

Ashley ⊹
Shepherd

To each of my kids,

Remi, Kanyon, Piney, and Bear. May your future homes always have an open door that all may enter to be fed and feel your love.

Contents

Introduction xiii

Kitchen Conversions xvii

Blissful Tips xix

Breakfast Bites 1

Egg Casserole Cups 3

Breakfast Energy Bites 4

Biscuits and Gravy 7

Sour Cream Pancakes 8

Fresh Whipped Cream 10

Buttermilk Syrup 11

French Toasties 12

Crepe Cups 15

Breakfast Burrito Pinwheels 16

Sweet Bites 19

Chocolate Chippers 21

Chewy Oatmeal Cookies 22

Sheps Cowboy Bites 25

Sugar Cookies 26

Gingersnaps 29

Peanut Butter Blossoms 30

Caramel Oat Bites 33

Apple Pie Bites 34

Brownie Bites 37

Chocolate Fudge Frosting 38

Cheesecake Shots 41

Lemon Cream Cheese Cake Bites 42

Strawberry Shortcake Biscuits 45

Cold Bites 47

Ranch Cheddar Cheese Ball Bites 48

Goat Cheese Bruschetta 49

Roasted Corn & Bacon Guacamole ... 50

Potato Salad 53

Wedge Salad Skewers 54

Summer Salad 57

Candied Pecans 58

Poppy Seed Dressing 59

Caesar Salad Cups 60

Chicken Salad Bites 63

Savory Bites 65

Stuffed Mushrooms 67

Spinach Artichoke Pinwheels 68

Chicken Cordon Bleu Bites 70

Parmesan Dijon Sauce 72

Beef Street Tacos 75

Chicken Street Tacos 76

Mini Stuffed Peppers 79

Honey Lime Enchilada Bites 80

Teriyaki Chicken Kabobs 83

Bread Bites 85

Mini Whole Wheat Bread 87

Mini White Bread Bites 88

Cinnamon Bites 91

Pumpkin Bites 92

Banana Bites 95

Parmesan Bites 96

Alfredo Dipping Sauce 99

Pretzel Bites 100

Warm Bites 103

Chicken and Rice Soup 105

Broccoli Cheese Soup 106

Roasted Corn Chowder 109

Tomato Basil Soup 110

GG's Chili 113

Comfort Bites 115

Sloppy Joe Sliders 117

BBQ Meatloaf 118

Crockpot Pot Roast 121

Garlic Mashed Potatoes 122

Baked Beans 125

Honey Roasted Yams 126

Chicken Pot Pies 129

Late Night Bites (Bonus Section) 131

Chex Crack 132

Popcorn Crunch 133

Hot Tamale Sweet Puff Corn 134

Street Corn Nachos 135

Acknowlegments 137

About the Author 138

About the Photographer 139

Introduction

When I was growing up, my parents gave me the most exquisite gifts, and they still do. They have a true talent when it comes to gift giving. Unfortunately, for my family and friends, I didn't inherit that gift.

I remember as a teenager being concerned about my future and what I had to offer the world. My senior year, I tried out for the most prestigious choir and made it. I can assure you it was not because of my singing talent. It was more for my outgoing personality and willingness to work. I will always be grateful for my choir teacher, Leanna Crockett, because it was only through choir that I found my real talent.

A group of my choir friends and I decided that every Sunday night we would pick a student from the high school and go sing a few songs to them. I decided to make a batch of cookies every time we went so we didn't look like complete weirdos when we showed up on someone's doorstep and wanted to sing to them. Cookies were our way into their home! As time went on, I realized I had no business being in this specific Sunday night quartet based on my vocal talent, but I did realize my place in the group. I was the treat giver. Word spread to other students and friends at school about "Ashley's Cookies," and everyone wanted a visit on Sunday night. I was hooked. I loved every minute of it. Bringing people cookies brought me fulfillment and joy.

After I graduated, I worked for a local catering company that helped me gain a better understanding and love for feeding large groups of people. One of my close friends came to me and asked if I would meet with her and her mom about some catering questions she had for her upcoming wedding. Before I knew it, I was volunteering to cater their entire wedding by myself! I knew I could do it. I just didn't know HOW I was going to do it.

That first wedding was the hardest one I've ever done. The beautiful outdoor summer evening decided to turn into a rain storm, causing us to move the food inside the house. People would walk through the garage, into the kitchen to visit the happy couple, and get their food off the counter.

Eventually the rain stopped. The hosts wanted the food back outside, so we gathered everything and took it out. It was complete chaos, and I remember being so in love with the entire scene—the people, the food, the chaos—everything. When I got home that night, I knew I had to start my own catering company.

Sheps Culinary Creations has taught me a lot in the past eight years. It has brought me so much joy. It's exactly what I have to offer the world. From large meals to blissful bites, each item is prepared with love. To all my readers, whatever your dream is, live it. Whatever your talent is, share it. For me, the reason I love feeding people is that every time I do, I give them a little piece of my heart, and you can too.

— Ashley

Kitchen Conversions

1 quart	=	2 pints	=	4 cups
1 pint	=	2 cups	=	16 ounces
1 cup	=	16 Tbsp.	=	8 ounces
¼ cup	=	4 Tbsp.	=	12 tsp.
1 Tbsp.	=	3 tsp.	=	½ ounce
A pinch	=	$\frac{1}{16}$ tsp.		
A dash	=	$\frac{1}{8}$ tsp.		
¼ cup	=	4 Tbsp.		
⅓ cup	=	5 Tbsp.		
½ cup	=	8 Tbsp.		
⅔ cup	=	11 Tbsp.		
¾ cup	=	12 Tbsp.		
1 cup	=	16 Tbsp.		

Blissful Tips

1. Instead of mincing fresh garlic, buy minced garlic in a jar at your local grocery store and you will always have it on hand.

2. You can purchase 40 percent fat heavy whipping cream at your local Costco store. It makes the difference.

3. Don't beat yourself up if not everything is made from scratch. If you don't want to make the biscuits but you want the gravy, purchase the biscuits or whatever else it is you need. The made-from-scratch items are better, but sometimes we just don't have the time.

4. Always buy pure vanilla extract, never imitation. It makes a difference!

5. Plan a party. Make the food. Party hard. Repeat.

Good morning

Sunshine!

Breakfast Bites

Egg Casserole Cups 3 • Breakfast Energy Bites 4

Biscuits and Gravy 7 • Sour Cream Pancakes 8

Fresh Whipped Cream 10 • Buttermilk Syrup 11

French Toasties 12 • Crepe Cups 15

Breakfast Burrito Pinwheels 16

Egg Casserole Cups

Ingredients

1 lb. ground sausage
18 large eggs
1½ cups milk
1 tsp. salt
1 tsp. pepper
1 bunch green onions (chopped)
1½ cups sharp cheddar cheese
12 slices white bread
1 (10.5 oz.) can cream of
    mushroom soup

Instructions

1. Preheat oven to 350 degrees and spray the cups in two muffin tins with nonstick cooking spray.

2. In a medium-sized skillet, cook the ground sausage. Drain off excess fat and set aside.

3. In a mixing bowl, whisk together the eggs, milk, salt, pepper, green onions, and cheddar cheese.

4. Using a small, round cookie cutter or knife, cut 24 even circles from the bread slices to fit in the bottom of each muffin cup in the tins.

5. Divide the egg mixture evenly between the 24 muffin cups (about ⅓ cup each) and sprinkle with the cooked sausage pieces.

6. Cover the muffin tins with plastic wrap and put them in the refrigerator overnight.

7. Top each casserole with 1 teaspoon cream of mushroom soup.

8. Bake until the eggs are set, 15 to 20 minutes. Let cool slightly to ensure the eggs are set before removing them from the pan to serve.

Full-Size Instructions

Spray a 9 x 13 baking pan with nonstick cooking spray. In a single layer, put the bread pieces face down. Pour egg mixture over the top and sprinkle with sausage pieces. Refrigerate overnight. Spoon cream of mushroom soup over the top just before baking. Bake at 350 degrees for 75 to 80 minutes.

❧ Breakfast Energy Bites ❧

Ingredients

6 Tbsp. butter
6 Tbsp. brown sugar
⅔ cup honey
1 tsp. vanilla extract
3 cups dry old-fashioned oats
2 Tbsp. chia seeds
2 cups Rice Krispies cereal
1 cup mini chocolate chips

Instructions

1. Spray a cookie sheet with nonstick cooking spray or line with parchment paper.

2. In a small pot over medium heat, add butter, brown sugar, and honey. Whisk on medium-low heat for 2 minutes until well combined. Remove from heat and add vanilla.

3. In a large mixing bowl, add the oats, chia seeds, and cereal. Pour the butter mixture over the cereal and mix together carefully until well combined. Let cool for 20 minutes.

4. Add mini chocolate chips and gently roll into balls. Refrigerate one hour.

Full-Size Instructions

Place mixture in a greased 9 x 13 baking pan and press down. Refrigerate 1 hour and cut into bars.

Biscuits and Gravy

Ingredients

Biscuits
2 cups flour
¼ tsp. baking soda
1 Tbsp. baking powder
1 tsp. salt
6 Tbsp. butter
1 cup buttermilk

Gravy
1 lb. ground sausage
½ cup flour
1 (12 oz.) can evaporated milk
3 cups whole milk
½ tsp. salt
¼ tsp. pepper

Instructions

1. Preheat oven to 400 degrees.

2. In a medium-sized bowl, combine 2 cups of flour, baking soda, baking powder, and salt. Using a pastry blender, cut the butter into the dry ingredients.

3. Fold in buttermilk until mixed. Do not overmix the dough. Sprinkle counter with flour and roll out dough to 1½ inches thick. Cut out 1-inch circles and place on greased cookie sheet. Bake 10 to 12 minutes or until golden brown.

4. In a frying pan, cook sausage until done. Leaving the meat and grease in the pan, sprinkle with ½ cup flour.

5. Cook until flour incorporates all of the grease. Add evaporated milk and whole milk and season with salt and pepper. Cook on low heat for 10 minutes or until mixture has thickened. Serve over biscuits.

Full-Size Instructions

Adjust the size of the biscuits to be 3 inches in diameter and bake for 15 to 17 minutes.

Notes

The biscuits are so easy to make; however, sometimes I am lazy and don't want to make them. I use Pillsbury biscuits every once in a while, and they work just fine. Don't beat yourself up if you don't make the biscuits. No one will ever know. The gravy is simple, but it can be tricky if you don't add the correct flour to milk ratio. I gauge this by the amount of grease that is in the pan after the sausage is done cooking. Sometimes I use ¾ cup of flour if I can tell there is too much grease after the ½ cup flour is added. The more you make it, the more you will be able to figure this out.

Sour Cream Pancakes

Ingredients

1 egg
1 cup buttermilk
½ cup sour cream
1¼ cups flour
2 tsp. baking powder
1 tsp. baking soda
½ tsp. salt
2 Tbsp. sugar
2 Tbsp. melted butter
Fresh fruit
Buttermilk Syrup
  (see recipe on page 11)
Fresh Whipped Cream
  (see recipe on page 10)

Instructions

1. Combine all wet ingredients in a mixing bowl and whisk until combined.

2. Add all of the dry ingredients to the wet ingredients.

3. Mix until just incorporated. Do not overmix.

4. Heat griddle to 350 degrees. Melt butter onto griddle.

5. Using a tablespoon, scoop batter into small circles, about 2 inches across.

6. Cook until little bubbles appear on the top of pancakes.

7. Flip over and cook the other side until golden brown.

8. When pancakes are cooked, top with Fresh Whipped Cream, fruit and Buttermilk Syrup.

Full-Size Instructions

Adjust the pancake size to 4 inches in diameter.

Notes

If you don't have buttermilk, make your own. In a bowl, combine 1 cup of milk and 1½ tablespoons white vinegar. Let it sit for 5 minutes.

Fresh Whipped Cream

Ingredients

2 cups heavy whipping cream
½ cup sugar
2 tsp. vanilla extract

Instructions

1. Place heavy cream, sugar, and vanilla into a mixer equipped with a whisk attachment.

2. Beat until stiff peaks form.

3. Store any unused whipped cream in an airtight container and keep in the fridge for up to 10 days.

⚘ Buttermilk Syrup ⚘

Ingredients

1 cup buttermilk
½ cup butter
1 cup white sugar
1 cup brown sugar
1 tsp. baking soda
1 tsp. vanilla extract

Instructions

1. Combine buttermilk, butter, and sugars in a saucepan. Boil for 1 minute.

2. Remove pan from heat and add baking soda and vanilla.

❦ French Toasties ❦

Ingredients

1 (8 oz.) pkg. brioche bread or
    Texas toast
4 eggs
¼ cup milk
1 tsp. vanilla extract
2 tsp. cinnamon
½ cup butter
½ cup powdered sugar
Fresh berries

Instructions

1. Slice bread into 1-inch-thick slices.

2. In a deep, wide bowl, whisk together eggs, milk, vanilla, and 1 teaspoon of cinnamon.

3. Preheat a large griddle to 350 degrees and coat with nonstick cooking spray.

4. Dip each slice of bread into the egg mixture (including the edges of the bread). Brioche is a great bread, because it will quickly absorb the egg mixture and will not break.

5. Place battered bread onto the griddle and cook for 3 to 4 minutes on each side until golden brown. Repeat with remaining bread.

6. When all of the bread slices are done cooking, cut the bread into four even rectangular pieces.

7. Cut the rectangular pieces into 12 even squares. Repeat with the remaining bread slices.

8. Melt butter in the microwave.

9. Sprinkle each square with powdered sugar and cinnamon and drizzle with melted butter.

10. Stack the squares 4 layers high and top them with a fresh berry. Add a party stick for easy serving at your next event.

Full-Size Instructions

Keep the brioche bread whole and layer it with powdered sugar and cinnamon and drizzle it with melted butter for the perfect breakfast.

❧ Crepe Cups ❧

Ingredients

Crepes
1½ cups milk
1¼ cups flour
3 large eggs
2 Tbsp. sugar
2 Tbsp. butter, melted
2 tsp. vanilla extract

Sweet Cream
1 (8 oz. pkg.) cream cheese,
   softened
1 cup sour cream
1 cup powdered sugar
2 cups fresh whipped cream
   (see recipe on page 10) or
   Cool Whip
2 tsp. almond extract

Fresh kiwi, blueberries, and
   raspberries

Crepe Instructions

1. In a bowl, combine the milk, flour, eggs, sugar, and melted butter.

2. Add vanilla and beat with a hand mixer until lumps are gone. (A blender works well too.)

3. Heat a small, lightly greased skillet.

4. Pour ¼ cup batter into the skillet and lift and tilt the pan to spread the batter thinly around the bottom of the skillet. Cook until light brown. Using a rubber utensil, carefully flip to the other side.

5. Carefully remove the crepe from the pan and repeat with the remaining batter.

6. Place muffin liners into a muffin tin and coat them with nonstick cooking spray.

7. Fit crepes into the liners, keeping the edges of the crepes ruffled.

8. Bake at 375 degrees for 10 to 15 minutes or until the crepe cups are set in place.

Sweet Cream Instructions

1. In a mixer with a paddle attachment, beat cream cheese, sour cream, and powdered sugar until smooth.

2. Fold in whipped cream and almond extract.

3. Fill crepe cups with sweet cream and fresh berries.

Full-Size Instructions

When crepes are cooked and removed from the skillet, fill with sweet cream and fresh berries. Roll filled crepes up into a burrito.

Breakfast Burrito Pinwheels

Ingredients

1 (17.25 oz.) pkg. puff pastry, thawed

¼ cup green scallions, chopped

4 oz. pepper jack cheese, shredded

6 large eggs, scrambled

6 slices of bacon, cooked and crumbled

½ cup breakfast sausage, cooked and crumbled

4 oz. sharp cheddar cheese, shredded

3 Tbsp. butter, melted

Instructions

1. Preheat oven to 350 degrees.

2. Turn the dough onto a floured surface and roll into a 12- by 18-inch rectangle.

3. Sprinkle with scallions and pepper jack cheese. Lightly press into the dough.

4. Sprinkle scrambled eggs and crumbled bacon and sausage evenly over the top.

5. Sprinkle with cheddar cheese.

6. Starting with the edge farthest away from you, roll up tightly into a log.

7. Cut dough roll into 12 even 2-inch pieces.

8. Arrange pinwheels evenly on a cookie sheet coated with nonstick cooking spray.

9. Bake 20 to 25 minutes or until golden brown.

10. Brush with melted butter.

Full-Size Instructions

Cut into 4-inch pieces and bake 30 minutes.

You are what you eat,
so eat something

Sweet.

Sweet Bites

Chocolate Chippers 21 • Chewy Oatmeal Cookies 22

Sheps Cowboy Bites 25 • Sugar Cookies 26

Gingersnaps 29 • Peanut Butter Blossoms 30

Caramel Oat Bites 33 • Apple Pie Bites 34

Brownie Bites 37 • Chocolate Fudge Frosting 38

Cheesecake Shots 41 • Lemon Cream Cheese Cake Bites 42

Strawberry Shortcake Biscuits 45

Chocolate Chippers

Ingredients

5 cups oatmeal
2 cups butter
2 cups brown sugar
2 cups sugar
4 eggs
1 Tbsp. vanilla extract
4 cups flour
2 tsp. salt
2 tsp. baking powder
1 Tbsp. baking soda
1 (12 oz.) bag semi-sweet
chocolate chips
1 (12 oz.) bag milk chocolate
chips

Instructions

1. Preheat oven to 350 degrees.

2. Measure oatmeal and blend it into a powder in a blender.

3. In a large mixing bowl, cream butter and sugars.

4. Add eggs and vanilla and mix until fluffy.

5. Add flour, salt, baking soda, baking powder, and oatmeal.

6. Add chocolate chips.

7. Drop by teaspoonfuls onto a greased cookie sheet and bake 6 to 7 minutes.

Full-Size Instructions

Place ¼ cup portions on a cookie sheet and bake 14 to 17 minutes.

Notes

It doesn't matter if you use quick or old-fashioned oats in this recipe since they will be ground up into a flour.

Chewy Oatmeal Cookies

Ingredients

1½ cups butter, melted and
  cooled
1½ cups brown sugar
1 cup white sugar
2 large eggs
1 Tbsp. vanilla extract
2 Tbsp. honey
1½ tsp. baking soda
½ tsp. salt
1 tsp. cinnamon
2⅔ cups flour
4½ cups old-fashioned oats
2 cups chocolate chips
½ cup raisins (optional)
½ cup chopped walnuts
  (optional)

Instructions

1. Preheat oven to 350 degrees.

2. In a mixer, beat butter and sugars until fluffy. Add eggs, vanilla, and honey and mix until combined.

3. Add baking soda, salt, cinnamon, and flour and mix just until combined. Add oats, chocolate chips, raisins, and walnuts.

4. Drop by teaspoonfuls onto a greased cookie sheet and refrigerate for at least an hour.

5. Bake for 6 to 7 minutes or until golden brown.

Full-Size Instructions

Place ¼ cup portions on a cookie sheet and bake 15 to 17 minutes.

Notes

The hardest part about this recipe is letting the dough sit in the fridge for an hour, but it really helps. If you get impatient like me and don't let it firm up in the fridge, it's not the end of the world, but they are more flat than I prefer.

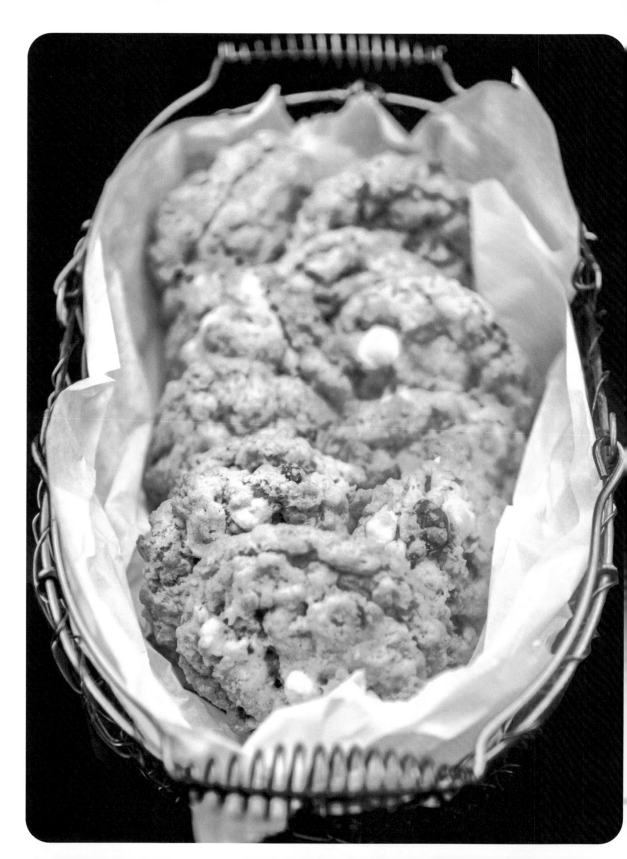

Sheps Cowboy Bites

Ingredients

1 cup butter
1 cup sugar
1 cup brown sugar
1 Tbsp. milk
1 Tbsp. vanilla extract
2 eggs
3 cups flour
1 tsp. baking soda
1 tsp. baking powder
1 tsp. salt
2 cups quick oats
2 cups cornflakes
1 cup semi-sweet chocolate chips
1 cup milk chocolate chips
1 cup white chocolate chips
1½ cups macadamia nuts, chopped

Instructions

1. Preheat oven to 350 degrees.

2. In a mixing bowl, cream together butter and sugars.

3. Add milk, vanilla, and eggs and mix until fluffy.

4. Add flour, baking soda, baking powder, and salt just until combined.

5. Stir in oats, cornflakes, chocolate chips, and nuts.

6. Drop by teaspoonfuls onto a lightly greased cookie sheet.

7. Bake 6 to 7 minutes or until golden brown.

Full-Size Instructions

Place ¼ cup portions on a cookie sheet and bake 15 to 17 minutes.

☙ Sugar Cookies ❧

Ingredients

Sugar Cookies
1 cup butter
¾ cup oil
1¼ cups sugar
¾ cup powdered sugar
2 eggs
3 Tbsp. water
5¼ cups flour
1 tsp. baking soda
1 tsp. cream of tartar
1 tsp. salt

Cream Cheese Frosting
1 (8 oz. pkg.) cream cheese
½ cup butter, softened
1 tsp. vanilla extract
4 cups powdered sugar
2 Tbsp. heavy cream

Sugar Cookie Instructions

1. Preheat oven to 350 degrees.

2. In mixer, combine butter, oil, and sugars.

3. Add eggs and water and beat until fluffy.

4. Add dry ingredients and mix until combined.

5. Using a 1-inch cookie scoop, place dough on a greased cookie sheet.

6. Dip the bottom of a drinking glass into a bowl of sugar and lightly press the top of each cookie with it.

7. Bake 5 to 7 minutes or until the bottoms are lightly brown. Do not overbake. If the cookie is golden brown, it's overbaked and will be dry.

8. Let cool and frost with cream cheese frosting.

Cream Cheese Frosting Instructions

1. Combine butter and cream cheese in a mixer and beat until smooth. Add vanilla and heavy cream. Add powdered sugar a cup at a time and beat until light and fluffy.

─ *Full-Size Instructions* ─

Using a 2-inch cookie scoop, place dough on a cookie sheet and bake 8 to 9 minutes.

─ *Notes* ─

This dough is perfect for cookie cutters as well. Roll dough between two sheets of parchment paper until 1/2-inch thick. Freeze for 20 minutes. Cut out and bake.

❖ Gingersnaps ❖

Ingredients

1½ cups butter, softened
1 cup sugar
1 cup brown sugar
½ cup molasses
2 eggs
4½ cups flour
1 Tbsp. baking soda
1 tsp. salt
1 Tbsp. ground ginger
2 tsp. ground cinnamon
1 tsp. ground cloves

Instructions

1. Preheat oven to 350 degrees.
2. In a mixing bowl, cream together butter and sugars.
3. Add molasses and eggs and mix until fluffy.
4. Add flour, baking soda, and salt just until combined.
5. Mix in ginger, cinnamon, and ground cloves.
6. Transfer the dough to an airtight container and refrigerate for 2 hours.
7. Scoop by teaspoonful and roll in sugar.
8. Place on a lightly greased cookie sheet.
9. Bake 6 to 7 minutes or until golden brown.

Full-Size Instructions

Scoop by tablespoonful and roll in sugar. Bake 8 to 9 minutes or until slightly cracked on top.

Notes

It is crucial that you follow the recipe with the refrigeration. The chilling of the dough helps the cookies keep their shape.

When baking, the cookies will start to crack on the top, and that's when you know they are done. Do not overbake!

⁂ Peanut Butter Blossoms ⁂

Ingredients

Peanut Butter Blossoms
1 cup butter
1 cup sugar
1 cup brown sugar
3 cups peanut butter
2 eggs
2 tsp. vanilla extract
2 cups flour
2 cups old-fashioned oats
1 tsp. baking soda
1 tsp. salt

Frosting
½ cup butter
¼ evaporated milk or heavy
  cream
2 tsp. vanilla extract
5 Tbsp. cocoa powder
3 cups powdered sugar

Instructions

1. Preheat oven to 350 degrees.

2. In a large bowl, cream together butter and sugars.

3. Add 1½ cups of the peanut butter, eggs, and vanilla.

4. Add flour, oats, baking soda, and salt.

5. Spray cookie sheet with nonstick cooking spray. Spread out dough in even layer.

6. Bake for 12 to 15 minutes or until light golden brown.

7. Melt remaining 1½ cups of peanut butter in the microwave.

8. Pour it over the top of the hot bars.

9. Let it cool until the peanut butter has set up.

10. While cooling, make the frosting by creaming the butter, milk (or heavy cream), and vanilla together and slowly adding the cocoa and sugar to them. Beat until creamy.

11. Cut out the bars using a 2-inch circle cookie cutter.

12. Using a piping bag with a star tip, begin in the center of each blossom and pipe in a circular motion toward the outside of each bar.

Full-Size Instructions

Keep bars on cookie sheet, frost, and cut into 3-inch bars.

❧ Caramel Oat Bites ❧

Ingredients

2 (11 oz.) bags caramel bits
1 (14 oz.) can sweetened condensed milk
1½ cups butter, melted
2 cups brown sugar
2 cups old-fashioned oats
2 cups flour
1 (12 oz.) bag chocolate chips

Instructions

1. Preheat oven to 350 degrees.

2. Spray a 9 x 13 baking pan with nonstick cooking spray and line it with parchment paper.

3. In a medium-sized saucepan, combine the caramel bits and sweetened condensed milk. Place over low heat and stir until smooth and creamy.

4. In a mixer, combine butter, brown sugar, oats, and flour.

5. Press half of the mixture into the prepared pan and bake it 8 to 10 minutes.

6. When the crust is done baking, spread the warm caramel over the entire bar.

7. Sprinkle chocolate chips over the caramel layer.

8. Using the rest of the dough, place small chunks of it on the chocolate chip layer.

9. Bake an additional 10 to 15 minutes or until golden brown.

10. Let cool and lift the baked bar out of the pan.

11. Cut into 1- by 1-inch squares.

Full-Size Instructions

Bake in 9x13 baking pan and cut into 3-inch bars.

⚘ Apple Pie Bites ⚘

Ingredients

Apple Pie Bites
2 (17.25 oz.) pkgs. puff pastry
2 (21 oz.) cans apple pie filling
¼ cup heavy cream or milk
½ cup course sugar

Salted Caramel
2 cups dark brown sugar
1 cup butter
1 (12 oz.) can sweetened
   condensed milk
⅔ cup dark corn syrup
¼ cup maple syrup
1 tsp. molasses
2 tsp. vanilla extract
½ tsp. salt

Instructions

1. Preheat oven to 400 degrees.

2. Set puff pastry on counter to thaw for 15 to 20 minutes.

3. Prepare the caramel by placing all of the ingredients into a medium-sized saucepan. Over medium heat, cook until the sugars have completely dissolved (10 to 15 minutes).

4. Set caramel aside to cool.

5. Cut each puff pastry sheet into 9 equal squares for a total of 36 squares.

6. Using a tablespoon, scoop an even amount of apple pie filling into each square.

7. Fold the square in half on the diagonal.

8. Seal each side of the triangle using a fork.

9. Brush with heavy cream and sprinkle with course sugar.

10. Bake 15 minutes or until golden brown.

11. Drizzle each triangle with salted caramel sauce.

Full-Size Instructions

Cut each puff pastry into 4 squares and use ¼ cup of apple pie filling in each square. Bake for 25 minutes.

Notes

This caramel can also be used for the most delicious caramel apples. After cooking it for the 15 minutes, attach a candy thermometer to the pan and continue to cook the caramel until it reaches 236 degrees, which should take another 10 to 12 minutes. Pour caramel into a bowl and let it rest. Cool it to 200 degrees before dipping the apples.

❧ Brownie Bites ❧

Ingredients

1¼ cups flour
½ tsp. salt
¾ tsp. baking powder
6 oz. unsweetened chocolate, chopped fine
12 Tbsp. butter
2¼ cups sugar
1 Tbsp. vanilla extract
4 eggs
1 cup chopped walnuts or pecans
Chocolate Fudge Frosting (see recipe on page 38)

Instructions

1. Preheat oven to 325 degrees.

2. Line a mini muffin tin with liners.

3. Spray each liner with nonstick cooking spray.

4. In a medium bowl, whisk together flour, salt, and baking powder.

5. Melt the chocolate and butter in a microwave safe bowl in 30-second increments until the mixture is completely smooth.

6. Gradually whisk sugar and vanilla into the chocolate mixture.

7. Add eggs one at a time, whisking after each addition.

8. Add flour mixture in 3 sections, folding in with rubber spatula.

9. Stir in nuts.

10. Add 1 tablespoon of batter to each mini muffin liner.

11. Bake for 12 to 15 minutes.

12. Let brownies cool for 2 hours. Take out of liners and frost with Chocolate Fudge Frosting.

Full-Size Instructions

Spray a 9x13 baking pan with nonstick cooking spray. Place two sheets of parchment paper into the pan; one long wise and one short wise, creating a leverage for the brownies to be removed easier. Spray the parchment paper with nonstick cooking spray. Pour batter in the pan and bake 30 to 35 minutes. Let cool for 2 hours and frost.

❧ Chocolate Fudge Frosting ❧

Ingredients

1½ cups butter, room
temperature
8 oz. melted bittersweet
chocolate bar
6 cups powdered sugar
2 tsp. vanilla extract
Dash of salt
¼ to ½ cup heavy cream

Instructions

1. Beat butter in mixer for 2 minutes or until light in color.

2. Melt chocolate bar in microwave in 20-second increments. Don't burn the chocolate!

3. Let chocolate cool and add to butter until combined.

4. Add powdered sugar slowly and then add vanilla.

5. Add heavy cream until desired thickness and beat on medium high for 1 minute.

Cheesecake Shots

Ingredients

Cream Cheese Filling
2 (8 oz.) pkgs. cream cheese, room temperature
⅓ cup sour cream
½ cup sugar
1 Tbsp. vanilla extract
Fresh Whipped Cream
(see recipe on page 10)
24 (2 oz.) plastic shot glasses
Assorted berries

Crust
1¼ cups crushed graham cracker crumbs
⅓ cup melted butter
¼ cup sugar

Instructions

1. In mixer, beat the cream cheese on medium high until smooth.

2. Add sour cream, ½ cup sugar, and vanilla.

3. Scrape down the sides of the bowl and mix until smooth.

4. In a separate mixer, or using a hand mixer, make the Fresh Whipped Cream.

5. Fold 1 cup of the Fresh Whipped Cream into the cream cheese mixture.

6. Refrigerate 1 hour.

7. To make the crust, mix graham crackers, melted butter, and ¼ cup sugar together.

8. Place 1 tablespoon of the crust into each shot glass.

9. Pipe 2 tablespoons of the cream cheese filling into the shot glasses and top with the additional whip cream.

10. Top with berries or sauce of choice.

Full-Size Instructions

Press the crust mixture into an 8-inch pie pan and bake it at 350 degrees for 10 minutes. Let it cool. Add the cream cheese mixture. Cover the pan with plastic wrap and place it in the fridge for 3 hours.

Lemon Cream Cheese Cake Bites

Ingredients

Cake Bites
1 box lemon cake mix
¾ cup buttermilk
1 cup sour cream
4 eggs
⅓ cup oil
2 tsp. lemon emulsion (or lemon extract)

Frosting
¼ cup butter, softened
4 oz. cream cheese
1 tsp. lemon extract
1 Tbsp. heavy cream
2 cups powdered sugar

Decoration
24 candy sticks
1 pkg. Wilton Candy Melts, bright white
1 pkg. sprinkles

Frosting Instructions

1. Combine butter and cream cheese in mixer and beat until smooth.

2. Mix in lemon extract and heavy cream.

3. Add powdered sugar a cup at a time and beat until light and fluffy.

Cake Bite Instructions

1. Preheat oven to 350 degrees.

2. Spray cookie sheet with nonstick cooking spray.

3. In a medium-sized mixing bowl, add all the cake ingredients.

4. Stir just until combined.

5. Pour the batter into the cookie sheet and bake it for 12 to 15 minutes until done.

6. Make the frosting while the cake is cooling.

7. When the cake has cooled, crumble it into fine crumbs in a medium-sized bowl. Add frosting.

8. Using your hands, mix the cake and frosting together until a dough forms. The mixture should be dense but not gooey.

9. Using a 2 tablespoon cookie scoop, scoop out the dough, packing it firmly into the scoop as you go.

10. Roll the dough in your hands, forming nicely shaped balls.

11. Melt white candy melts in the microwave using 20 second increments. Don't let it burn!

12. Dip the sticks into the melted candy and put them into the cake balls.

13. Set the cake pops on a cookie sheet and place in freezer for 15 minutes.

14. Place melted candy melts into a glass mug. (Melt them again if necessary.) Dip a cake pop into the mug and evenly coat it with the melted candy.

15. Let the coating drip off and run to the bottom of the cake pop.

16. Roll the cake pop in the decorative sprinkles while the candy on it is still melted.

17. Repeat with all cake pops.

Full-Size Instructions

Pour the batter into a 9 x 13 baking pan. Bake at 350 degrees for 25 minutes and frost.

Notes

Fun thing about this recipe is you can use any colors or flavors. If you want to use a chocolate cake mix, you can. Just use the chocolate fudge frosting recipe. If you want to add sprinkles, do it when the candy melts are still warm so the sprinkles will stick to the cake pop.

Strawberry Shortcake Biscuits

Ingredients

2 cups flour
¼ tsp. baking soda
1 Tbsp. baking powder
2 Tbsp. sugar
1 tsp. salt
6 Tbsp. butter
1 cup buttermilk
½ cup coarse sugar
1 (1 lb.) pkg. fresh strawberries
½ cup sugar
Fresh Whipping Cream
 (see recipe on page 10)
Vanilla bean ice cream

Instructions

1. Preheat oven to 400 degrees.

2. In a medium-sized bowl, combine 2 cups of flour, baking soda, baking powder, sugar, and salt. Using a pastry blender, cut the butter into the dry ingredients.

3. Fold in the buttermilk. Do not overmix the dough. Sprinkle the counter with flour and roll out the dough to 1½ inches thick. Cut out 1-inch circles and place them on a greased cookie sheet.

4. Heavily coat each biscuit with coarse sugar.

5. Bake 10 to 12 minutes or until golden brown.

6. While the biscuits are baking, cut off the tops of the strawberries and place them in a blender.

7. Add the sugar and pulse, leaving the strawberries in chunks.

8. Make the Fresh Whipped Cream.

9. When the biscuits are cooled, cut them in half and add 2 tablespoons of the strawberry mixture, a dollop of whip cream, and a small scoop of vanilla bean ice cream.

Full-Size Instructions

Cut the biscuits into 3-inch circles. Bake 15 to 17 minutes. Using two full biscuits, add ⅓ cup strawberry mixture, ¼ cup whipped cream, and a large scoop of vanilla bean ice cream.

A party without
food
is just a meeting.

Cold Bites

Ranch Cheddar Cheese Ball Bites 48 • Goat Cheese Bruschetta 49

Roasted Corn & Bacon Guacamole 50 • Potato Salad 53

Wedge Salad Skewers 54 • Summer Salad 57

Candied Pecans 58 • Poppy Seed Dressing 59

Caesar Salad Cups 60 • Chicken Salad Bites 63

Ranch Cheddar Cheese Ball Bites

Ingredients

- 2 (8 oz.) pkgs. cream cheese
- 1 (1 oz.) packet of ranch seasoning mix
- 1 cup shredded cheddar cheese
- ¼ cup green onions, chopped
- 1 tsp. garlic powder
- 1 tsp. Worcestershire sauce
- 2 cups pecan pieces
- 24 mini pretzel sticks

Instructions

1. In a mixer, combine cream cheese, ranch seasoning, cheddar cheese, green onions, garlic powder, and Worcestershire sauce until combined.

2. Shape into 1-inch balls and roll the balls in the pecan pieces.

3. Cover in plastic wrap and refrigerate at least 2 hours.

4. Place one pretzel in each cheese ball just before serving.

— Full-Size Instructions —

Shape cheese mixture into one round ball and roll it in the pecan pieces. Cover and refrigerate for 2 hours. Serve with crackers.

Goat Cheese Bruschetta

Ingredients

1 (8 oz.) pkg. goat cheese
1 pkg. assorted grape or cherry tomatoes (red, yellow, orange) cut in half
1 baguette cut into ¼-inch slices
6–8 fresh basil leaves, julienned
4–5 Tbsp. bottled balsamic glaze
4–5 Tbsp. butter
Salt
Pepper

Instructions

1. Preheat oven to 400 degrees.

2. To make what is called crostini, arrange the baguette slices on the cookie sheet. Spread butter evenly on each slice. Toast in the oven for 5 to 6 minutes.

3. Spread goat cheese on the cooled crostini slices.

4. Top the crostini slices with tomatoes and chopped basil.

5. Drizzle with balsamic glaze.

Roasted Corn & Bacon Guacamole

Ingredients

1 cup sweet corn
7–8 ripe avocados
1 small onion, chopped
8 slices bacon, cooked and chopped
2 Roma tomatoes, cubed
1 tsp. minced garlic
2–3 tsp. cumin
1 tsp. garlic salt
Salt
Pepper
Torilla chips
2 Tbsp. fresh lime juice
12 (5 oz.) plastic martini glasses

Instructions

1. Preheat oven to 400 degrees.

2. Spread the corn on a cookie sheet and put it in the oven for 10 minutes or until golden brown. The goal is to achieve some char on the corn and blacken parts of it. Remove it from the oven and set it aside.

3. Peel and pit the avocados. Mash them with a fork in a medium-sized bowl.

4. Add the onion, cooked bacon, tomatoes, and seasonings. Add the cooled corn and mix.

5. Place the tortilla chips in a bowl and pour the fresh lime juice over them. Gently toss them with your hands to incorporate the juice.

6. Serve the guacamole with the tortilla chips in plastic martini glasses.

Full-Size Instructions

Serve the guacamole in a medium-sized mixing bowl.

Potato Salad

Ingredients

10 small potatoes
5 hard-boiled eggs, peeled and
    diced
6 dill pickles, sliced
1–1½ cups mayo
Salt
Pepper
Fresh parsley

Instructions

1. Preheat oven to 400 degrees.

2. Pierce the potatoes with a fork and bake them for one hour.

3. Cut the potatoes in half.

4. Carefully spoon out the potatoes and cut them into small cubes. Set aside the empty potato skins.

5. In a medium-sized bowl, combine potatoes, diced hard-boiled eggs, pickles, and mayo. If the mixture is too dry, and a little more mayo.

6. Salt and pepper to taste.

7. Spoon the potato mixture back into the empty potato skins and top with fresh parsley.

Full-Size Instructions

Serve the potato salad in a large mixing bowl.

Notes

This recipe is so simple, and it reminds me so much of my childhood. Every gathering we had as a family we ate this potato salad. Every time I eat it I am reminded of my family—past, present, and future.

Wedge Salad Skewers

Ingredients

1 head iceberg lettuce,
    chopped into small wedges
½ lb. Swiss cheese, cubed
½ lb. bacon, cooked and sliced
1 pkg. mushrooms, sliced
1 red onion, chopped into
    quarters
1 pkg. grape tomatoes
1 bottle ranch dressing
24 (6-inch) wooden skewers

Instructions

1. Put the lettuce, cheese, bacon, mushroom, onions, and tomato on the skewers.

2. Drizzle ranch dressing over the top of each salad wedge.

Full-Size Instructions

Serve salad in a large mixing bowl.

⚜ Summer Salad ⚜

Ingredients

1 head romaine lettuce, washed
  and chopped
2 cups baby spinach
½ lb. strawberries, sliced
¾ cup Candied Pecans
  (see recipe on page 58)
½ cup feta cheese
1 pear, peeled and sliced
Poppy Seed Dressing
  (see recipe on page 59)

Instructions

1. In a large mixing bowl, combine romaine lettuce and baby spinach.

2. Divide the lettuce and spinach evenly and place in martini glasses.

3. Divide the toppings evenly and place them on the lettuce and spinach in the martini glasses.

4. Drizzle Poppy Seed Dressing over the top.

Full-Size Instructions

Serve salad in a large mixing bowl.

⚜ Candied Pecans ⚜

Ingredients

1 cup sugar
¼ cup water
2 tsp. cinnamon
2 cups pecans
2 tsp. vanilla extract

Instructions

1. In a frying pan, combine sugar, water, and cinnamon.

2. Over medium heat, cook until mixture comes to a boil.

3. Add pecans and continue to cook for about 3 minutes, stirring to coat every pecan.

4. Remove from heat and add vanilla.

5. Spread pecans on parchment paper to cool.

6. When nuts have cooled, chop into pieces.

Poppy Seed Dressing

Ingredients

1½ cups oil
½ cup sugar
¾ cup red wine vinegar
¾ tsp. dry mustard
2 Tbsp. red onion, diced
1½ tsp. salt
1 Tbsp. poppy seeds

Instructions

1. Combine the first 6 ingredients in a blender.

2. When frothy, add the poppy seeds.

3. Store in the fridge for up to 2 weeks.

Caesar Salad Cups

Ingredients

4 cups fresh shredded Parmesan cheese
1 head romaine lettuce, cut into thin strips
1 (5 oz.) pkg. seasoned croutons, chopped
1 cup Caesar salad dressing
Salt
Pepper

Instructions

1. Preheat oven to 400 degrees.

2. Line a baking sheet with parchment paper.

3. Scoop one heaping tablespoon of cheese onto the baking sheet and pat down slightly. Repeat until there are 12 mounds on the sheet.

4. Bake for 5 to 7 minutes or until the cheese is bubbly and slightly golden.

5. Remove from the oven and let cool for 1 minute. Gently remove the discs from the baking sheet and lay them on an upside down muffin tin to form cups.

6. Let the cups cool completely before removing them from the muffin tin.

7. In a large mixing bowl, combine the lettuce, croutons, and remaining cheese.

8. Toss the salad with Caesar dressing.

9. Salt and pepper to taste.

10. Fill each cheese cup with the salad.

11. Garnish with extra croutons.

Full-Size Instructions

In a large bowl, combine all the ingredients and toss them until the Caesar dressing has been incorporated. Salt and pepper to taste. Serve immediately.

Chicken Salad Bites

Ingredients

1 (24 oz.) pkg. wonton wrappers
2 large chicken breasts, cooked, cooled, and diced
1 cup chopped celery
1½ cups halved red grapes
¾ cup slivered almonds
1 gala apple, diced
3 green onions, chopped
1½ cups mayo
Salt
Pepper

Instructions

1. Place 2 wonton wrappers in each regular-sized muffin tin. Spray the wonton wrappers with nonstick cooking spray and bake according to package.

2. Let the wonton wrappers cool.

3. In a medium-sized bowl, combine the chicken, celery, grapes, almonds, apple, 2 green onions, mayo, salt, and pepper.

4. Scoop the chicken mixture into the wonton cups and garnish with the remaining green onion.

Full-Size Instructions

Instead of using wonton wrappers, place the chicken salad in freshly baked croissants.

Laughter

is brightest
where food is best.

Savory Bites

Stuffed Mushrooms 67 • Spinach Artichoke Pinwheels 68

Chicken Cordon Bleu Bites 70 • Parmesan Dijon Sauce 72

Beef Street Tacos 75 • Chicken Street Tacos 76

Mini Stuffed Peppers 79 • Honey Lime Enchilada Bites 80

Teriyaki Chicken Kabobs 83

Stuffed Mushrooms

Ingredients

2 pkgs. white mushrooms
1 (12 oz.) pkg. Jimmy Dean
   ground sausage
1 medium onion, chopped
2 tsp. minced garlic
Salt
Pepper
1 (8 oz. pkg.) cream cheese,
   softened
¾ cup grated Parmesan cheese

Instructions

1. Preheat oven to 375 degrees.

2. Remove all the stems from the mushrooms so you are only left with the tops.

3. Chop the stems up into small pieces and place them in a medium-sized bowl.

4. Brown the sausage in a frying with chopped onion. Add garlic and salt and pepper to taste.

5. Remove the sausage from the heat and add it to the stems.

6. Stir in cream cheese and ½ cup Parmesan cheese.

7. Place the tops of the mushrooms facing up on a cookie sheet.

8. Fill each top with the sausage mixture until full. Sprinkle with remaining Parmesan cheese.

9. Bake 20 minutes or until golden brown.

Notes

I always buy minced garlic in a jar. That way you don't have to mince it yourself, and you always have it when you need it! I use about 1 teaspoon for every clove a recipe calls for.

Spinach Artichoke Pinwheels

Ingredients

1 (8 oz. pkg.) cream cheese
1 (20 oz.) jar of marinated
 artichoke hearts, drained and
 chopped
½ cup mayo
½ cup grated Parmesan cheese
2 tsp. minced garlic
1 (10 oz.) bag of frozen
 chopped spinach

1 (17.25 oz.) pkg. puff pastry,
 cool but not frozen

Instructions

1. Preheat oven to 350 degrees.

2. In a medium-sized bowl, combine all of the ingredients and mix until smooth.

3. Place one sheet of the puff pastry on a floured surface. Spread a think layer of the spinach mixture on the pastry and roll it up.

4. Repeat with remaining sheets.

5. Cut into 1-inch pinwheels. Bake for 12 minutes or until golden brown.

Full-Size Instructions

Eliminate the puff pastry. Place the spinach mixture in a 9 x 9 baking pan and bake for 20 minutes. Serve with crackers or bread.

Chicken Cordon Bleu Bites

Ingredients

1 (16 oz.) can refrigerated
crescent rolls
12 slices deli ham
12 pieces frozen popcorn
chicken
1¼ cups Parmesan Dijon Sauce
(see recipe on page 72)
1 cup shredded Swiss cheese
1 bunch fresh parsley

Instructions

1. Preheat oven to 375 degrees.

2. Spray the 12 cups of a regular-sized muffin tin with nonstick cooking spray.

3. Remove the dough from the can. Combine the rolls into one large sheet and press the seams together, making an 8- by 8-inch rectangle.

4. Cut the dough into 12 squares.

5. Press the squares into the cups of the muffin tin.

6. Place one slice of ham in the bottom of each muffin cup.

7. Place one piece of popcorn chicken on top of the ham and 2 tablespoons of Parmesan Dijon on top of the chicken.

8. Sprinkle with shredded Swiss cheese.

9. Bake 15 to 18 minutes or until golden brown.

10. Garnish with fresh parsley.

— Notes —

It's difficult to know if cordon bleu is cooked all the way through. I check for a couple of things: 1. Using a meat thermometer, I check the inside center of the meat. If the temperature is between 160 and 165, the meat is done. 2. If the tops are golden brown and the Swiss cheese is starting to bubble out of the cordon bleu, it's a good sign that it's done.

Full-Size Recipe

Full-Size Recipe Ingredients

> 8 chicken breasts
> 8 slices of ham
> 16 slices of Swiss cheese
> 3 eggs
> 2 tsp. water
> 2 cups Italian breadcrumbs
> 2 tsp. fresh thyme
> Salt
> Pepper

Full-Size Recipe Instructions

1. Preheat oven to 400 degrees.

2. Pound the chicken flat or butterfly it.

3. Layer each breast with ham and cheese.

4. Roll up the chicken breasts and set them aside.

5. In a small bowl, combine and beat together the eggs and water.

6. In a separate bowl, mix the breadcrumbs with the thyme and add salt and pepper to taste.

7. Dip the chicken in the egg mixture and then coat it with breadcrumbs. Place it on a greased cookie sheet.

8. Bake for 25 minutes or until completely baked all the way through.

Parmesan Dijon Sauce

Ingredients

½ cup butter
2 tsp. minced garlic
¼ cup flour
1 pint heavy cream
1 cup fresh Parmesan cheese
2 Tbsp. Dijon mustard
½ tsp. salt
¼ tsp. pepper

Instructions

1. In a small saucepan over medium heat, melt the butter and garlic.

2. Add flour to the melted butter, whisk, and allow to cook for 3 to 4 minutes.

3. Pour in heavy cream and whisk to incorporate.

4. Continue to cook until the mixture bubbles and begins to thicken.

5. Add cheese, mustard, and salt and pepper.

6. Remove from heat.

❧ Beef Street Tacos ❧

Ingredients

3 lbs. chuck roast
5 tsp. minced garlic
1 chipotle pepper in adobo sauce
   (2 if you want it more spicy)
4 oz. roasted chopped green
   chilies.
1 white onion, chopped
3 limes, juiced
2 bay leaves
1 Tbsp. cumin
1 Tbsp. oregano
2 tsp. salt
1 tsp. pepper
½ cup beef stock

36 street-size flour tortillas
1 green apple, shredded
½ white onion, sliced thin
½ cup queso fresco cheese,
   crumbled
½ cup crème fresh (½ cup sour
   cream and the zest and juice
   of 1 lime)
36 mini clothespins (optional)

Instructions

1. Combine the first twelve ingredients in a crockpot and cook on low for 8 to 10 hours.

2. After 8 hours, remove the bay leaves and shred the meat.

3. Serve on street-size flour tortilla shells (which are smaller than regular-sized tortillas) and top with shredded green apple, thinly sliced onion, queso fresco cheese, and crème fresh.

4. Use the clothespins to hold the tortillas closed once they are filled. (See the photo on the opposite page.) You can purchase these online or at various craft stores.

Notes

The two ingredients that make these tacos extra delicious are the shredded green apple and the thinly sliced onion. Place the thinly sliced onion in a bowl of water and let it soak overnight. It takes the bite out of the onion, and you are left with a perfect crunch!

❧ Chicken Street Tacos ❧

Ingredients

1½ lbs. boneless, skinless
  chicken thighs
3 Tbsp. olive oil
½ tsp. salt
½ tsp. pepper

2 tsp. cumin
1 tsp. smoked paprika
½ tsp. chili powder
1 tsp. onion powder

12 street-size corn tortillas
1 cup Pico de Gallo
2 avocados, sliced
½ cup queso fresco cheese
1 cup shredded lettuce
½ cup crème fresh (½ cup sour
  cream and the zest and juice
  of 1 lime)
12 mini clothespins

Instructions

1. Preheat oven to 375 degrees.

2. Place the chicken on a cookie sheet and drizzle it with olive oil. Season it with salt and pepper.

3. Roast the chicken for 20 minutes and set it aside.

4. When the chicken has cooled, shred the meat and add the seasonings.

5. Serve on street-size corn tortillas (which are smaller than regular-sized tortillas) and top with Pico de Gallo, sliced avocado, queso fresco cheese, shredded lettuce, and crème fresh.

6. Use the clothespins to hold the tortillas closed once they are filled. (See the photo on the opposite page.) You can purchase these online or at various craft stores.

Notes

Place the cooked chicken in a mixer, add seasonings, mix, and the meat will shred instantly. It's so easy to do it this way, and you can do it while the chicken is still hot.

Mini Stuffed Peppers

Ingredients

1 lb. ground hamburger
1 pkg. taco seasoning
1 (15 oz.) can black beans, drained
1 cup sweet corn
6 oz. diced green chili
1 cup rice, cooked
4 oz. cream cheese
12 mini peppers (red, yellow, orange)
1½ cups shredded Mexican cheese
Cilantro sauce

Instructions

1. Preheat oven to 350 degrees.
2. Cook the hamburger in a large frying pan.
3. Drain the fat and add the taco seasoning. Set aside.
4. In a large bowl, combine beans, corn, chilies, and rice.
5. Add meat and cream cheese and mix until smooth.
6. Fill each pepper with meat mixture and place it on a cookie sheet.
7. Top with shredded cheese.
8. Bake for 20 to 25 minutes or until the peppers are soft.
9. Top with cilantro sauce.

Full-Size Instructions

Fill 6 regular-sized peppers with the meat mixture and bake for 45 minutes.

Honey Lime Enchilada Bites

Ingredients

1 rotisserie chicken, shredded
⅓ cup honey
¼ cup lime juice (about 5 limes)
2 tsp. minced garlic

1 (16 oz.) can mild green
  enchilada sauce
¾ cup heavy cream
Marinade sauce from the
  chicken

24 mini flour tortillas
2 cups shredded Mexican
  cheese blend
Fresh cilantro

Instructions

1. In a medium-sized bowl, combine the chicken, honey, lime juice, and garlic. Stir to combine. Set in the fridge to marinate for at least 30 minutes.

2. Preheat the oven to 375 degrees. Spray a 12-count muffin tin with nonstick cooking spray and place the tortillas in the cups of the tin.

3. In another bowl, combine and mix together the enchilada sauce, the cream, and the marinade sauce from the chicken.

4. Place ½ teaspoon of the above mixture in each tortilla shell. Add 1 tablespoon of the chicken and ½ teaspoon of the mixture on top of the chicken. Sprinkle cheese on the enchiladas.

5. Bake for 15 to 20 minutes until bubbly and light golden brown.

6. Garnish with fresh cilantro.

Full-Size Instructions

Place a layer of the enchilada sauce mixture on the bottom of a 9 x 13 baking pan. Using full-sized flour tortillas, place the chicken in the tortillas, top the chicken with cheese, roll up the tortillas, and place them in the baking pan. Garnish with remaining cheese and sauce. Bake for 30 to 35 minutes.

Teriyaki Chicken Kabobs

Ingredients

1½ lb. boneless, skinless chicken thighs
1 cup soy sauce
1 cup sugar
½ cup pineapple juice
2 Tbsp. minced garlic
3 Tbsp. fresh ginger, minced
1 bunch green onion, chopped

24 (6-inch) wooden skewers
2 red onions cut into 1-inch chunks
1 fresh pineapple cut into 1-inch chunks

2 Tbsp. cornstarch
4 Tbsp. water

Instructions

1. Place the chicken thighs in a gallon-sized sealable bag.
2. Combine the soy sauce, sugar, pineapple juice, garlic, ginger, and green onion and pour it over the chicken.
3. Refrigerate chicken in sauce overnight.
4. Place the wooden skewers in a shallow dish and cover with water. Let sit on the counter overnight, or at least for an hour before grilling.
5. After marinating, cut the chicken into 1-inch chunks. Save the marinade!
6. In an alternating pattern, put the onion, pineapple, and chicken on the skewers.
7. Preheat grill to medium heat.
8. Place excess marinade in a medium-sized saucepan and heat over medium heat until boiling.
9. Combine water and cornstarch in a small bowl.
10. Pour cornstarch mixture into the boiling marinade and stir for 1 minute or until thickened.
11. Remove it from the heat and let it cool.
12. Grill the skewers for 10 to 12 minutes until the chicken is cooked to 165 degrees.
13. Brush the skewers with the thickened marinade sauce.

Full-Size Instructions

Keep chicken thighs whole and grill for 15 to 20 minutes or until chicken reaches 165 degrees.

Cut pineapple and red onion into 1-inch slices and grill.

Happiness is the
smell of fresh baked
bread!

Bread Bites

Mini Whole Wheat Bread 87 • Mini White Bread Bites 88

Cinnamon Bites 91 • Pumpkin Bites 92

Banana Bites 95 • Parmesan Bites 96

Alfredo Dipping Sauce 99 • Pretzel Bites 100

❧ Mini Whole Wheat Bread ❧

Ingredients

4 cups warm water
3 Tbsp. instant yeast
3 Tbsp. dough enhancer
¼ cup vital wheat gluten
1 Tbsp. salt
¾ cup olive oil
¾ cup honey
11–12 cups freshly ground hard white wheat flour
3–4 Tbsp. butter

Instructions

1. In a mixer with a dough hook, mix together water, yeast, dough enhancer, gluten, salt, oil, and honey. Let rest for at least 10 minutes.

2. Add in 6 cups of flour and combine until smooth. Let rest for at least 5 minutes.

3. Add the remaining flour a cup at a time until, as you mix it, you notice it pulling away from the bowl (at cup 5 or 6).

4. Let rest for 10 minutes, and then remove the dough from the mixer and divide and shape it into 12 equal loaves. Place the loaves in 12 greased mini loaf pans.

5. Let the dough rise for 25 to 30 minutes. Bake the bread at 350 degrees for 15 minutes.

6. Take the loaves out of the oven and brush the tops with butter.

Full-Size Instructions

Divide the dough into 3 greased loaf pans. Let it rise 30 to 45 minutes and bake it at 350 degrees for 20 minutes.

Notes

Nothing is better than fresh-baked bread and butter! A few tips to help your bread turn out perfect: 1. The water should be hot enough to activate the yeast but not too hot that you kill it. I know my temperature is right if I can run my hand under the water and it's hot to the touch but not hot enough that I cannot keep my hand in the water. 2. You have to use dough enhancer! I buy mine at the local grocery store, but you can easily make it. Dough enhancer is like a conditioner for the bread and keeps it soft and light. 3. You will notice a difference if you grind your own wheat; however, 100 percent whole wheat flour or white flour would work. 4. Your biggest temptation with wheat bread will be to keep adding flour. Tell yourself to be patient. Wheat flour takes longer than white to absorb the water, so let the dough mix for a few minutes before you add more flour. If you add too much, the dough will be tough and hard to handle. The dough should be sticky to the touch but easy to handle.

Mini White Bread Bites

Ingredients

3 cups warm water
2 Tbsp. active dry yeast
⅔ cup honey
7½ cups bread flour
4 Tbsp. melted butter
1 Tbsp. salt

Instructions

1. In a large mixing bowl, combine 3 cups warm water, yeast, ⅓ cup of the honey, and 3½ cups of the flour. Mix until combined. Cover and let rest for 30 minutes.

2. Add 3½ cups more of the flour, the remaining honey, the melted butter, and the salt.

3. Knead for 5 minutes. Add the remaining ½ cup flour if the dough is still sticky. (Should be slightly sticky but not sticky enough to cling to your hands.)

4. Place the dough in a greased bowl and cover.

5. Let rise until doubled, about 30 minutes.

6. Grease 6 mini bread pans and divide and shape the dough.

7. Place the dough into the pans and let it rise until doubled.

8. Bake at 350 degrees for 20 minutes.

9. Brush tops of loaves with butter.

Full-Size Instructions

Divide and shape the dough and place it into 3 full-sized bread pans. Bake for 30 minutes.

Cinnamon Bites

Ingredients

Dough

1 cup warm water
3 Tbsp. yeast
½ cup sugar
2 cups whole milk
½ cup butter
2 eggs
2 tsp. salt
1 (3.5 oz.) pkg. instant vanilla
   pudding
9 cups bread flour

Cinnamon Mixture

1 Tbsp. cinnamon
1½ cups brown sugar
1 cup butter

Cream Cheese Frosting

½ cup butter, softened
1 (8 oz. pkg.) cream cheese,
   softened
1 tsp. vanilla extract
4 cups powdered sugar
⅛ tsp. salt
2 Tbsp. heavy cream

Instructions

1. In a small bowl, combine warm water, yeast, and 1 tablespoon of the sugar. Let sit until yeast is bubbly.

2. In a small saucepan, combine milk with ½ cup butter. When the butter is melted, turn off the heat and set the milk mixture aside until it is cool to the touch.

3. In a mixer using the whisk attachment, beat the eggs until fluffy.

4. Add the eggs to the cool milk mixture. Mix in the salt and the remaining sugar.

5. Combine the milk mixture and the yeast mixture.

6. Add the dry pudding and mix.

7. Add flour one cup at a time until the dough is soft and easy to handle.

8. Put the dough into a large greased bowl and let it rise for 1 hour.

9. Place the dough on a floured surface and roll it out into a rectangular shape.

10. Blend together 1 Tbsp. cinnamon and 1½ cups brown sugar.

11. Spread 1 cup of butter over the dough and sprinkle it with the combined cinnamon mixture. Lightly press into the dough.

12. Roll up the dough and slice it into discs.

13. Place rolls on a cookie sheet and let them rise for another 30 to 45 minutes.

14. While the rolls are rising, combine the frosting ingredients in a mixer and beat until smooth.

15. Bake at 350 degrees for 18 to 20 minutes or until golden brown. Top with Cream Cheese Frosting.

❧ Pumpkin Bites ❧

Ingredients

2 cups flour
1 tsp. baking soda
2 tsp. cinnamon
½ tsp. salt
1 cup sugar
¼ cup butter
2 eggs
1½ cups canned pumpkin
½ cup plain Greek yogurt
1 tsp. vanilla extract
1 cup mini chocolate chips

Instructions

1. Preheat oven to 350 degrees.

2. Combine flour, baking soda, cinnamon, and salt.

3. Place sugar and butter in mixer and beat until well blended.

4. Add eggs, pumpkin, yogurt, and vanilla.

5. Add flour mixture and mix just until blended.

6. Fold in chocolate chips.

7. Grease 6 mini loaf pans and line with parchment paper.

8. Spoon batter evenly into pans.

9. Bake for 30 to 35 minutes or until a toothpick inserted comes out clean.

Full-Size Instructions

Spoon batter into 2 full-sized loaf pans and bake for 1 hour.

⚘ Banana Bites ⚘

Ingredients

¼ cup sugar
1 tsp. cinnamon

¾ cup butter
3 cups sugar
3 eggs
7 bananas, ripe and mashed
1 (16 oz.) container sour cream
1 Tbsp. vanilla extract
2 tsp. cinnamon
1 tsp. salt
1 Tbsp. baking soda
4½ cups flour
1 cup chopped walnuts
  (optional)
1 cup mini chocolate chips
  (optional)

Instructions

1. Preheat oven to 300 degrees.

2. Grease 8 mini loaf pans.

3. In a small bowl, stir together ¼ cup sugar and 1 teaspoon cinnamon.

4. Lightly dust the inside of each loaf pan with the sugar and cinnamon mixture.

5. In a large bowl, cream together butter and 3 cups sugar.

6. Mix in eggs, mashed bananas, sour cream, vanilla, and cinnamon.

7. Mix in salt, baking soda, and flour.

8. Stir in nuts and chips (optional).

9. Divide into pans.

10. Bake 35 minutes or until a toothpick comes out clean.

Full-Size Instructions

Grease 4 regular loaf pans, divide batter evenly, and bake for 1 hour.

⚘ Parmesan Bites ⚘

Ingredients

3 cups water
2 Tbsp. yeast
½ cup sugar
2 tsp. salt
1 cup melted butter
2 eggs (whisked together)
6–7 cups bread flour
1 cup grated Parmesan cheese
2 Tbsp. parsley
1 Tbsp. garlic powder
Alfredo Dipping Sauce
   (see recipe on page 99)

Instructions

1. In a small mixing bowl, combine 1 cup of the warm water, the yeast, and 1 tablespoon of the sugar. Let activate for 5 minutes.

2. In a large mixing bowl, add the remaining 2 cups of hot water, the remaining sugar, and the salt.

3. Slowly incorporate ½ cup of the melted butter and the eggs into the water, sugar, and salt mixture.

4. Add in the yeast mixture.

5. Add the flour, one cup at a time, until it's fully incorporated. The dough should be slightly sticky but not sticky enough to cling to your hands.

6. Let the dough rise for 1 hour.

7. On a floured surface, roll the dough to a 1-inch thickness.

8. Cut into 1-inch strips and then into 1-inch squares.

9. In a small bowl, combine the grated cheese, parsley, and garlic powder.

10. Dip each square into the remaining ½ cup of melted butter and roll them in the cheese mixture.

11. Let rise for 30 minutes.

12. Bake at 350 degrees for 8 to 10 minutes.

13. Dip the bites in Alfredo Dipping Sauce.

⸎ Full-Size Instructions

Cut the dough into 2- by 3-inch rectangles. Dip them in the butter and roll them in the cheese mixture. Let rise for 45 minutes and bake for 15 minutes.

Alfredo Dipping Sauce

Ingredients

½ cup butter
2 Tbsp. minced garlic
2 cups 40% fat heavy whipping cream
1 cup grated fresh Parmesan cheese
Salt
Pepper
1 tsp. Italian seasoning

Instructions

1. In a medium-sized saucepan, add the butter and garlic.

2. Whisk until the butter is melted.

3. Add heavy cream and whisk until smooth.

4. Add the grated Parmesan and simmer for 4 to 5 minutes until the cheese is incorporated into the liquid and the liquid has thickened.

5. Season with salt, pepper, and the Italian seasoning.

6. Serve with Parmesan Bites.

Notes

This sauce is the same recipe I use for my Chicken Alfredo. Double the recipe, use it over fettuccine noodles, and dinner is served!

⚜ Pretzel Bites ⚜

Ingredients

3 cups flour
1 Tbsp. brown sugar
1 Tbsp. yeast
½ tsp. salt
3 Tbsp. butter, melted
1 cup milk
½ cup water

2 cups water
4 Tbsp. baking soda
1 egg
1 tsp. water
3 Tbsp. coarse sea salt
2 Tbsp. butter, melted

Instructions

1. Combine the flour, brown sugar, yeast, and salt in a medium-sized bowl.

2. Add 3 tablespoons melted butter, milk, and water.

3. Knead for 5 minutes.

4. The dough should be smooth and just barely sticky to your fingers.

5. Let the dough rise until doubled.

6. Preheat oven to 450 degrees.

7. Turn the dough onto a slightly floured surface and roll into a 2-inch-thick rope.

8. Cut into 1-inch strips.

9. Place the pretzel bites on a lined baking sheet and let them rise for 15 minutes.

10. In a medium-sized saucepan, boil 2 cups of water with 4 tablespoons baking soda. Once the baking soda is mostly dissolved, take the mixture off the heat.

11. Place each pretzel bite in the baking soda bath for 2 minutes.

12. Carefully put each pretzel bite onto a greased baking sheet.

13. Combine the egg and water. Brush each piece with the egg wash and sprinkle them with salt.

14. Bake for 10 to 12 minutes or until golden brown.

15. Brush the pretzel bites with 2 Tbsp. melted butter.

Full-Size Instructions

When you roll out the dough into a rope, instead of cutting it into 1-inch strips, cut it into 20-inch pieces. Curve the ends of each rope to make a circle. Cross the ends at the top. Twist the ends once and lay them over the bottom of the circle. Repeat with the remaining dough. Let rise and bake for 20 minutes.

Cooking is *love* made visible.

Warm Bites

  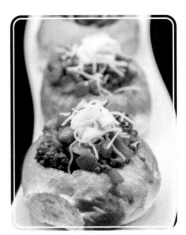

Chicken and Rice Soup 105 • Broccoli Cheese Soup 106

Roasted Corn Chowder 109 • Tomato Basil Soup 110

GG's Chili 113

❧ Chicken and Rice Soup ❧

Ingredients

4 chicken breasts
1 large onion, chopped
1 (10 oz.) bag shredded carrots
10 celery stalks, chopped
5 tsp. minced garlic
1 tsp. sage
1 tsp. thyme
1 tsp. rosemary
3 Tbsp. chicken base
Salt
Pepper
9 cups chicken stock

8 Tbsp. butter
½ cup flour
4–5 cups heavy cream
3 cups rice, cooked

Instructions

1. Place the chicken in a stockpot with water and cook it over medium high heat for 15 minutes. Remove it from the heat and let it cool.

2. When the chicken is cool, shred it into small pieces.

3. Place the onion, carrots, celery, and seasonings in 9 cups of chicken stock. Let simmer until vegetables are tender.

4. In a saucepan, melt the butter and add the flour. Cook until the mixture is golden brown.

5. Slowly add the heavy cream and whisk until smooth. Season with salt and pepper.

6. Add the heavy cream mixture to the vegetable mixture. Stir in the rice.

7. Serve in small 2-ounce shot glasses.

Full-Size Instructions

Serve soup in regular-sized bowls.

Notes

This is my all-time favorite soup recipe. Let me share a few tips with you: 1. After the vegetables are tender, I like to use a emulsion blender and chop the vegetables very small, almost baby food like. (Some people prefer the veggies chopped, so that's why I didn't include this part in the instructions.) 2. The longer you let the roux mixture (butter and flour) cook, the better the flavor. I cook my roux golden to dark brown before I add in the heavy cream. 3. I interchange rice and noodles in this recipe all the time. Just make sure that regardless of what starch you use, cook it before adding it to the soup mixture.

⚜ Broccoli Cheese Soup ⚜

Ingredients

5 Tbsp. butter
1 large onion, diced
3 tsp. minced garlic
¼ cup flour
2 cups vegetable stock
3 cups heavy cream
4 cups broccoli florets, diced
    into small pieces
3 large carrots, peeled and
    sliced very thin
1 tsp. salt
1 tsp. pepper
1 tsp. smoked paprika
¾ tsp. dry mustard
8–12 oz. shredded sharp
    cheddar cheese

Instructions

1. In a medium-sized saucepan, add butter and diced onion and sauté over medium heat until onion is soft.

2. Add garlic and flour.

3. Slowly add in vegetable stock and heavy cream.

4. Stir in broccoli, carrots, and seasonings. Let simmer for 20 to 25 minutes.

5. When the soup has simmered for 20 minutes, add in 8 ounces of shredded cheese and simmer for an additional 10 to 15 minutes or until smooth and thick.

6. Pour into 2-ounce shot glasses and garnish with the remaining 2 ounces of cheese.

— Full-Size Instructions —

Serve soup in regular-sized bowls.

— Notes —

My words of advice for this recipe are simply this: Don't forget the smoked paprika! Adding the paprika takes this recipe from an 8 to a 10 in a matter of seconds. When you are allowing the soup to simmer, keep it on a low heat to prevent scorching on the bottom of the pan. Dairy and high heat are a no go! You won't regret making this recipe. It is so good!

Roasted Corn Chowder

Ingredients

1 large zucchini, cubed
2 cups sweet corn
8 Tbsp. butter
1 large onion, diced
1 (10 oz.) bag shredded carrots
10 celery stalks, chopped
5 tsp. minced garlic
½ cup flour
9 cups water
3 Tbsp. chicken base
2 tsp. salt
1 tsp. pepper
3 large potatoes, peeled,
    boiled, and cubed.
4–5 cups heavy cream

Instructions

1. Chop zucchini into cubes and place on cookie sheet with corn. Roast in 400 degree oven for 10 to 15 minutes or until golden brown with a few char marks. Set aside.

2. In a large pot, add butter, diced onion, carrots, and celery and sauté over medium heat until onion is soft.

3. Add garlic and flour.

4. Add the water to a large pot and whisk in the chicken base to make chicken stock.

5. Slowly add the chicken stock and the seasonings to the vegetable mixture. Let simmer for 20 to 25 minutes.

6. When the soup has simmered for 20 minutes, add zucchini, corn, potatoes, and heavy cream. (Set aside some of the corn for garnish.) Simmer for an additional 10 to 15 minutes.

7. Pour into miniature bowls and garnish with extra roasted corn and fresh parsley.

Full-Size Instructions

Serve soup in regular-sized bowls.

Notes

This recipe is so fun, because you can add whatever you want to it! When we have fresh vegetables from the garden, I'll throw in a squash here and there. If I have leftover corn on the cob, I'll cut it off the cob and roast fresh corn. You can add red, russet, or golden yellow potatoes, and the recipe is to die for.

⚜ Tomato Basil Soup ⚜

Ingredients

2½ fresh basil
1 cup slivered almonds
1 cup Parmesan cheese
5 tsp. garlic
1½ cups olive oil
3 tsp. salt
1 cup butter
2 large onions, chopped
8 stalks celery, chopped
3 tsp. oregano
7 (14.5 oz.) cans stewed
   tomatoes
1 quart heavy cream

Sour cream
Tortilla strips
Parsley

Instructions

1. Combine the first six ingredients into a blender until smooth.

2. In a large pot, melt the butter and add the onion and celery. Sauté until the onions are transparent.

3. Add oregano and tomatoes. Cook on low heat for 6 to 8 hours.

4. Make soup smooth by using an emulsion blender.

5. Stir in heavy cream.

6. Serve in 2 oz. shot glasses and garnish with sour cream, fresh tortilla strips, and parsley. It's also especially delicious served with toasted cheese sandwiches.

Full-Size Instructions

Serve soup in regular-sized bowls and top with sour cream, tortilla strips, and parsley.

Notes

The first items that you will put in the blender are the ingredients to create a pesto sauce. Do not skimp on the basil. I have found that it usually is cheaper to buy the whole basil plant at the store instead of buying 4 to 5 of the small packages of fresh basil. You can make this in a crockpot on low for 8 hours, or to quicken the cooking time, throw it all in a pressure cooker and it will be done in about 5 minutes. You will not believe the results! If you love tomato soup, this recipe will not let you down.

You can also buy canned pesto sauce at your local grocery store. For this recipe, add 2 cups pesto.

❧ GG's Chili ❧

Ingredients

1 lb. ground hamburger
1 large onion, chopped
1 large green pepper, diced
4 tsp. minced garlic
2 Tbsp. oil
3 Tbsp. chili powder
1 tsp. oregano
1 tsp. garlic powder
1½ tsp. salt
½ tsp. cumin
2 (14.5 oz.) cans diced or
    stewed tomatoes
3 (30 oz.) cans pinto beans
12 small round rolls

Sour cream
Shredded cheese

Instructions

1. In a large pot, combine hamburger, onion, pepper, garlic, and oil. As the meat cooks, add in the seasonings.

2. When the hamburger is brown, add tomatoes and beans. Cook on low for at least one hour.

3. Cut off the tops of the rolls and hollow out the centers.

4. Serve the chili in the rolls and top with sour cream and shredded cheese.

Full-Size Instructions

Cut off the tops and hollow out the centers of large bread bowls and scoop the chili into them. Top with sour cream and shredded cheese.

All food is *Comfort* food.

Comfort Bites

Sloppy Joe Sliders 117 • BBQ Meatloaf 118

Crockpot Pot Roast 121 • Garlic Mashed Potatoes 122

Baked Beans 125 • Honey Roasted Yams 126

Chicken Pot Pies 129

Sloppy Joe Sliders

Ingredients

12 slider buns
Olive oil
Poppy seeds
1 lb. ground beef
1 Tbsp. butter
½ green bell pepper, minced
½ yellow onion, minced
2 Tbsp. minced garlic
2 Tbsp. tomato paste
⅓ cup ketchup
2 Tbsp. brown sugar
1 tsp. yellow mustard
2 tsp. Worcestershire sauce
Salt
Pepper
¼ cup water
12 wooden skewers

Instructions

1. Preheat oven to 350 degrees.

2. Place slider buns on a baking sheet and drizzle with olive oil and top with poppy seeds.

3. Toast in oven for 5 to 7 minutes until lightly browned.

4. Heat a large skillet over medium heat and add meat.

5. Cook meat until browned and remove from pan and drain excess fat.

6. Add butter to the pan and sauté the bell pepper and onion for 3 to 4 minutes until soft.

7. Add garlic and continue to cook for another minute.

8. Add beef back into the skillet and add tomato paste.

9. Next, add ketchup, brown sugar, mustard, Worcestershire, salt, pepper, and water.

10. Stir well and cook until thickened, about 10 minutes.

11. Remove from heat and add a generous portion to each bun. Place a skewer through the center of each slider.

Full-Size Instructions

Place a generous amount in 6 large-sized buns.

❧ BBQ Meatloaf ❧

Ingredients

6 slices bacon
2 Tbsp. olive oil
1 onion, chopped
2 lbs. ground hamburger
2 eggs
1 tsp. minced garlic
1 tsp. salt
½ tsp. pepper
2 tsp. Worcestershire sauce
1 (10 oz). can tomato sauce or ketchup
¾ cup quick oats
1 Tbsp. onion powder

Brown Sugar Glaze
½ cup ketchup
4 Tbsp. brown sugar
1 Tbsp. mustard

Instructions

1. Preheat oven to 350 degrees.

2. Cut bacon into small pieces.

3. In a large frying pan, combine oil, onion, and bacon. Cook until bacon is crispy. Set aside.

4. In a medium-sized bowl, mix hamburger, eggs, and seasonings. Mix well.

5. Add tomato sauce and oats.

6. Fold in onion and bacon.

7. Divide meat evenly into 24 balls.

8. Place in muffin tins and bake for 15 minutes.

9. Drain off excess fat and spread brown sugar glaze evenly over the top.

10. Bake another 15 minutes.

Full-Size Instructions

Place meat in regular-sized loaf pan. Bake at 350 degrees for 35 minutes. Spread brown sugar glaze evenly over the top. Bake another 20 minutes.

Crockpot Pot Roast

Ingredients

4 Tbsp. butter
3–4 lbs. beef roast
Seasoning salt
Pepper
1 large onion, chopped
1 pkg. sliced mushrooms
1 (10.5 oz.) can beefy mushroom
   soup
1 (10.5 oz.) can golden
   mushroom soup
1 (10.5 oz.) can beef consommé
2 tsp. minced garlic
Garlic Mashed Potatoes
   (see recipe on page 122)
50 plastic appetizer spoons
Gravy pipettes

Gravy
Salt
Pepper
2 Tbsp. cornstarch

Roast Instructions

1. Melt the butter in a large frying pan. Place a thawed roast in the pan and season it with salt and pepper. Rotate the roast so that each side gets browned and seasoned.

2. Place the roast in a crockpot. Top with onions, mushrooms, soups, and garlic. Cook on low for 12 to 14 hours.

3. After making the mashed potatoes, place one tablespoon of them on plastic appetizer spoons and top with pieces of the shredded meat.

4. Garnish with fresh parsley and a gravy pipette.

Gravy Instructions

1. Remove liquid from crockpot and reduce down in saucepan for 10 to 15 minutes. This will boil off excess water and concentrate the flavor of the gravy.

2. Add salt and pepper to taste.

3. Combine 3 tablespoons of water and 2 tablespoons of corn starch in a cup or small bowl. Slowly whisk the mixture into the gravy. If the gravy isn't thick enough, repeat the cornstarch steps.

Full-Size Instructions

Serve the roast and potatoes as a full entrée.

Garlic Mashed Potatoes

Ingredients

8–10 Yukon gold potatoes,
  diced and boiled
½ cup butter, melted
1 Tbsp. minced garlic
1 cup heavy cream
1 cup fresh Parmesan cheese
Salt
Pepper

Instructions

1. Bring a large pot with water to a boil and cook potatoes until tender.

2. In a separate saucepan, combine butter, garlic, and heavy cream. Simmer on low heat for 10 minutes. Remove from heat and set aside.

3. When the potatoes are done, drain the water and transfer them to a large bowl.

4. Pour the cream mixture over the potatoes.

5. Add the cheese and mash everything together until combined.

6. Salt and pepper to taste.

❧ Baked Beans ❧

Ingredients

- 8 slices bacon, sliced into small pieces
- 1 medium onion, diced
- 3 (15 oz.) cans pork and beans, drained
- 3 Tbsp. mustard
- ½ cup brown sugar
- 2 Tbsp. Worcestershire sauce
- 50 plastic appetizer spoons
- ½ cup onion straws
- 2 Tbsp. fresh parsley

Instructions

1. In a large skillet, cook bacon and onion until onions are translucent and bacon is lightly crisp.

2. Open canned beans. Remove the liquid and the "pork" piece.

3. Pour beans into bacon and onion mixture.

4. Add mustard, sugar, and Worcestershire sauce.

5. Simmer over medium-low heat for 30 minutes.

6. Place 2 tablespoons of bean mixture in plastic appetizer spoons and top with onion straws and parsley.

Full-Size Instructions

Scoop beans into a large serving dish and top with onion straws and parsley.

Honey Roasted Yams

Ingredients

3 medium yams, washed,
    peeled, and diced
4 Tbsp. honey
4 Tbsp. olive oil
1 Tbsp. cinnamon
Salt
Pepper

Instructions

1. Preheat oven to 400 degrees.

2. Put diced yams into a gallon-size Ziploc bag. Add honey, oil, cinnamon, and a pinch of salt and pepper. Close the bag and shake it until the seasonings have covered the yams.

3. Remove from bag and arrange the yams in a single layer on a greased cookie sheet.

4. Bake for 20 minutes and then flip the yams over. Bake for another 15 to 20 minutes or until the yams are tender and golden brown.

Full-Size Instructions

Cut the yams in half and drizzle them with the sauce mixture. Bake at 400 degrees for 30 minutes.

Notes

These make a perfect healthy side dish for dinner. I could devour a whole pan. I call them Honey Roasted Yams, because that's what they really are! They are not sweet potatoes, so when you go to the store, make sure you buy yams. Tip: don't allow a lot of extra marinade on the cookie sheet, because it tends to burn.

⚛ Chicken Pot Pies ⚛

Ingredients

Filling
1 cup butter, softened
¼ cup flour
1 Tbsp. cornstarch
½ cup milk
1 onion, chopped
1 bag shredded carrots
2 celery stalks, chopped
1 Tbsp. fresh garlic
1 cup chicken broth
½ tsp. thyme
½ rosemary
Salt
Pepper
2 medium-sized baked chicken
   breasts, cubed
½ cup frozen peas

Pie Crust
4 sheets puff pastry
1 egg, beaten

Instructions

1. Preheat oven to 375 degrees.
2. Prepare the filling by combining 4 tablespoons of the softened butter with the flour in a bowl. Set aside.
3. In a separate bowl, combine the cornstarch and milk.
4. In a medium-sized saucepan, add 4 tablespoons of the butter and sauté the onion, carrot, celery, and garlic over medium high heat for 5 minutes.
5. Add the chicken broth and bring to a boil. Cover and simmer for 10 minutes or until vegetables are tender.
6. Add the butter and flour mixture and bring to a simmer, constantly stirring.
7. Pour in the milk and cornstarch mixture and stir until combined.
8. Add the thyme, rosemary, and salt and pepper to taste.
9. Stir in the chicken and peas.
10. Let mixture cool to room temperature.
11. Using prepared puff pastry, roll out the dough onto a floured surface and cut in 2-inch circles.
12. Spoon the chicken mixture on one side of each circle and top with another circle of puff dough. Press the edges together with a fork to secure.
13. Repeat until all of the pastry and filling is used up.
14. Brush pastry pies with egg wash and sprinkle with salt and pepper.
15. Bake for 20 to 25 minutes until puffed up and golden brown.

Full-Size Instructions

Pour the filling into a glass 9-inch pie pan or glass casserole dish. Place puff pastry sheet over the top of the dish. Brush with egg mixture, top with salt and pepper, and bake 20 to 25 minutes until puffed up and golden brown.

Eat.

Sleep.

Snack.

Repeat.

Late Night Bites
(Bonus Section)

Chex Crack 132 • Popcorn Crunch 133

Hot Tamale Sweet Puff Corn 134 • Street Corn Nachos 135

Chex Crack

Ingredients

- 3 cups Rice Chex cereal
- 3 cups Corn Chex cereal
- 3 cups Golden Grahams cereal
- 1½ cups sliced almonds
- 2 cups sweetened coconut
- 1 cup sugar
- 1 cup corn syrup
- 1 cup butter
- 1 tsp. vanilla extract

Instructions

1. In a large mixing bowl, toss together cereals, nuts, and coconut.

2. In a medium-sized saucepan, combine sugar, corn syrup, and butter.

3. Bring mixture to a boil and let boil for 2 minutes.

4. Remove from heat and stir in vanilla.

5. Pour sugar mixture over cereal and stir to evenly coat.

6. Store in an airtight container.

Popcorn Crunch

Ingredients

3 quarts popped corn
1⅓ cups pecan halves
1 cup butter
1 cup corn syrup
1 cup sugar
½ tsp. cream of tarter
1 tsp. baking soda
1 Tbsp. vanilla extract
4 cups mini marshmallows
   (frozen)
1 cup mini chocolate chips

Instructions

1. In a large bowl, combine popcorn and pecans.

2. In a medium-sized saucepan, combine butter, corn syrup, and sugar.

3. Stir mixture until it comes to a boil. Let boil for 10 minutes.

4. Remove from heat and stir in cream of tarter, baking soda, and vanilla.

5. Pour over popcorn mixture and stir.

6. Stir in frozen marshmallows and chocolate chips.

7. Spread onto buttered cookie sheet to cool.

❧ Hot Tamale Sweet Puff Corn ❧

Ingredients

1 cup butter
1½ cups sugar
½ cup corn syrup
1 tsp. vanilla extract
8 cups mini marshmallows
8 oz. puffed corn
2 cups hot tamales

Instructions

1. In a medium-sized saucepan, heat butter, sugar, and corn syrup until boiling.

2. Boil for 3 minutes and remove from heat.

3. Stir in vanilla and mini marshmallows until marshmallows are almost melted.

4. In a large mixing bowl, pour sugar mixture over puffed corn.

5. Add hot tamales and put mixture on wax paper to cool for one hour.

Street Corn Nachos

Ingredients

- 3 cups corn (frozen, fresh, or canned)
- ¼ cup mayo
- 2 tsp. chili powder
- 1 tsp. smoked paprika
- Juice and zest of 1 lime
- Salt
- Pepper
- 1 (11 oz.) bag tortilla chips
- 1 (8 oz.) pkg. shredded sharp cheddar cheese
- 1 cup cojita cheese, crumbled
- ½ cup sour cream
- ½ cup chopped cilantro leaves

Instructions

1. Preheat oven to 400 degrees. Coat a baking sheet with nonstick cooking spray.

2. In a large bowl, combine corn, mayo, chili powder, paprika, lime juice, lime zest, and season with salt and pepper.

3. Place tortilla chips in a single layer on a prepared baking sheet. Top with half of the cheeses and all of the corn mixture.

4. Sprinkle the remaining cheese on the top.

5. Place in the oven and bake for 10 to 15 minutes or until the cheeses have melted.

6. Drizzle with sour cream and garnish with cilantro leaves.

Acknowledgments

Mom and Dad, thank you for always believing in my crazy ideas and helping me turn them into a reality. Thank you for being my biggest food critics and for helping me strive to be my best self. You're the best cheerleaders a daughter could ask for.

Thank you to my sweet siblings for listening to me ramble about idea after idea and for helping me narrow down the best recipes to put in this book. You all are my safe place, and I love you.

My best friend and photographer Amanda: You are the greatest friend I could have ever hoped for. Thank you for being patient with me, for learning with me, and for helping me accomplish everything I undertake. You are my soul sister.

My sweet husband: You are the peanut butter to my jelly. The milk to my donut, and the steak to my mashed potatoes. You have always given me wings to fly. Thank you for loving all of me and for pushing me to dream bigger. You are the greatest blessing in my life. I'm gonna love you one day past forever, but that's as far as it goes.

The Savior of the world, Jesus Christ: Only through Him all hopes and dreams are made possible. He has blessed me with so many opportunities and has given me the strength to keep going when times are hard.

About the Author

Ashley Shepherd grew up in Mapleton, Utah, where her love of food began with simply taking cookies to friends and neighbors every Sunday.

Ashley continued her education at Brigham Young University where she received a bachelors degree in family home and consumer science. She taught at Orem Junior High School, and then at Salem Hills High School where she taught foods and implemented the Pro Start Program there.

In 2012, Ashley left teaching behind to launch Sheps Culinary Creations, a full-service catering company located in Spanish Fork, Utah. Ashley is passionate about creating delicious food that brings people together for any occasion. You can see more of her work at www.shepsculinarycreations.com.

About the Photographer

Amanda Youd grew up in the beautiful Heber Valley and grew to love the amazing atmosphere that the canyon provides. Amanda thinks life is all about slowing down, loving people, laughing big, and eating delicious food. Photography has given her the opportunity to do that and to share that happiness with others.

Amanda loves to serve others and is passionate about capturing priceless moments for families and friends to enjoy forever. Amanda currently resides in Spanish Fork, Utah, with her husband and three children. You can see Amanda's work on Instagram @capturethisbyjo.